The Wonder of
BEAVERS

To all kids who love beavers, and to Dr. Richard Coles,
a grown-up who loves beavers.

— Patricia Corrigan

**For a free color catalog describing Gareth Stevens Publishing's list of high-quality
books and multimedia programs, call 1-800-542-2595 (USA) or 1-800-461-9120 (Canada).
Gareth Stevens Publishing's Fax: (414) 332-3567.**

Library of Congress Cataloging-in-Publication Data available upon request from publisher.
Fax: (414) 332-3567 for the attention of the Publishing Records Department.

ISBN 0-8368-2661-2

First published in North America in 2000 by
Gareth Stevens Publishing
A World Almanac Education Group Company
330 West Olive Street, Suite 100
Milwaukee, WI 53212 USA

This edition is based on the book *Beavers for Kids* © 1996 by Patricia Corrigan, with illustrations
by John F. McGee, first published in the United States in 1996 by NorthWord Press, Inc.,
Minocqua, Wisconsin, and published as *Beaver Magic for Kids* in a library edition by Gareth
Stevens, Inc., in 1996. Additional end matter © 2000 by Gareth Stevens, Inc.

Photographs © 1996: Mike Barlow/Dembinsky Photo Associates, Cover; Tom and Pat Leeson, 7, 8,
15, 16-17, 26, 28-29; Len Rue, Jr., 10-11, 36, 39; Jen and Des Bartlett/Bruce Coleman, Inc., 18-19,
21; Jonathan T. Wright/Bruce Coleman, Inc., 27; Skip Moody/Dembinsky Photo Associates, 31;
Dominique Braud/Dembinsky Photo Associates, 33; Jim Brandenburg/Minden Pictures, 40;
F-Stock, Inc., 44-45; Leonard Lee Rue III, 46-47.

Printed in the United States of America

1 2 3 4 5 6 7 8 9 04 03 02 01 00

The Wonder of
BEAVERS

by Amy Bauman and Patricia Corrigan
Illustrations by John F. McGee

Gareth Stevens Publishing
A WORLD ALMANAC EDUCATION GROUP COMPANY

If you hike through the woods near the end of the day, you might be lucky enough to spot a very busy and hard-working creature. If you see a large, dark animal swimming in the water, it could be a beaver!

Beavers are mammals that live along rivers, lakes, and ponds in North America and Europe. They like both water and land.

Beavers are best known for the dams they build in their watery habitats.

Beavers are rodents, like squirrels and mice. Beavers grow to be about 4.5 feet (1.4 meters) long, and weigh between 40 and 60 pounds (18 and 27 kilograms). They can live ten years or more. Beavers are nocturnal — they rest during the day and are active at night.

A beaver's fur is like a waterproof jacket. A thick, outer coat of silky fur protects an inner layer of dense, woolly fur. Oil on the fur helps keep water out so beavers stay dry. Long ago, people hunted beavers for their soft, shiny fur. Beavers almost became extinct.

A beaver's tail is flat, shaped like a paddle, and covered with scales. It can grow to be 12 inches (30 centimeters) long.

When beavers
swim, they
steer with
their tails.
They also slap
the surface
of the water
with their
tails. Beavers
may "talk"
to each other
this way.

Beavers paddle through water with their strong back feet. They can swim about 2 miles (3 kilometers) an hour. They can stay underwater for a long time, too.

A clear layer of tissue covers a beaver's eyes. This layer protects the beaver's eyes, like goggles, while it swims.

Baby beavers are called
kits. They are born in
late spring.

A female beaver usually has four kits. A kit is about 9 inches (23 cm) long and weighs less than 1 pound (0.5 kg). Each kit is born with fluffy fur, a tiny tail, and big front teeth. The teeth, called incisors, can grow to almost 2 inches (5 cm) long!

Beavers are some of nature's best builders. They build dams in rivers, marshes, and lakes. Some dams can be 12 feet (3.7 m) high and 600 feet (183 m) long. That's as long as two football fields!

Beavers build their dams
out of tree branches, stones,
and mud.

To build dams,
beavers cut
down trees
by gnawing
them with
their incisors.
Then they
bite off the
tree branches
and drag
them into
the water.

Beavers usually work alone. Sometimes, however, beaver families, called colonies, will work together on big projects. A colony is made up of an adult male, an adult female, and their newest litter.

Often, a beaver colony lives together in a home called a lodge. The lodge is made of sticks and mud. Each lodge has one big room.

Inside the lodge, beavers build the floor above the water to keep it dry, and they cover the floor with soft grasses. The colony sleeps here. Beavers go in and out of the lodge through tunnels. They also escape from enemies through these tunnels.

Some people think beavers harm the environment because they cut down too many trees. Other people believe beavers are helpful to the environment. Beaver dams are homes for other animals. Dams can also stop a stream from drying up, or land from eroding.

Beavers don't use trees just for building — they like to eat them, too! They also eat shrubs and water plants. Beavers eat about 2 pounds (1 kg) of food every day.

Beavers spend most of their time building dams and lodges and gathering food. They also spend time grooming.

A beaver may spend as much as an hour a day grooming! It uses all four paws like combs to get rid of tangles.

Each of a beaver's front paws has five "fingers." Each finger has a sharp claw for digging and holding food and other objects. Each back paw has five toes, but only two claws. All five toes on each back paw are webbed, like a duck's feet.

Besides
building,
eating, and
grooming,
beavers do
something
extra special
together.
They play!
Look at
this beaver
splash!

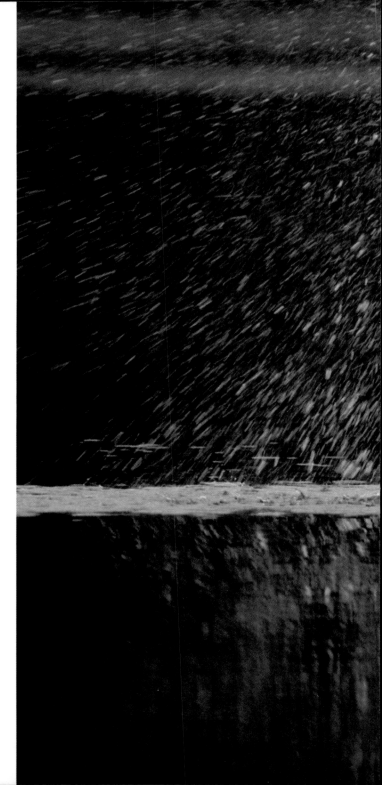

The beaver
is a clever
and useful
creature.
You would
be lucky
to spot a
busy beaver
someday!

Glossary

dam – a wall-like structure that holds back water

environment – the natural surroundings of an area or habitat

eroding – wearing or washing away due to wind, water, or ice

extinct – no longer alive

habitats – the places where animals and plants live in nature

incisors – special cutting teeth often found in mammals, especially rodents

litter – the young from one birth

mammals – animals with hair or fur that feed their young with mother's milk

rodents – a group of gnawing mammals, including mice, squirrels, and beavers

webbed – connected by skin

Index